SEX IT UP, Reality TV Show

by Katherine Kane

With over 20 different sex scenes, 'Sex It Up, Reality TV Show' is a behind the scenes look at a TV programme and all that goes on both behind and in front of the cameras. The idea for the show came to Katherine Kane, producer and main character in the book, when she met Ian, a male porn star. The book follows them on a journey to new erotic horizons and sexual discoveries, as well as giving insight into the various phases and difficulties encountered during the production of a reality show. Readers get to follow auditions and the live final before the winner is announced.

ISBN: 978-1-291-50243-5

eBook ISBN: 978-1-291-50177-3

Chapters

A Busy Friday

"I told you to come up with a different type of reality TV show, not the same rubbish re-hashed over again! If that is too difficult, perhaps you should think about looking for another job!"

That was the last thing my boss said to me before I went home one Friday night. Not a great way to start the weekend, especially as I had no other bright ideas that had not already been done.

At home I sat down to a lonely, despondent dinner, feeling depressed and worried. Depressed because I had believed I had a bright future with the television company, and worried as I had just bought a house and had a large mortgage to pay.

Things were not looking good, but in an attempt to cheer myself up I decided to go out and paint the town. Anything was better than sitting here, alone, feeling miserable, so I put on my shortest skirt, highest shoes and favourite top, and set off for the biggest and liveliest disco in town.

I was only there about five minutes, and had not yet found any of my friends, (who I knew would be there), nor had I had time to get a drink, when the sexiest man I had seen in ages appeared in front of me and asked, with a knowing look, if I wanted a drink.

"Your house or mine?" was my only reply.

"Whichever you prefer," he replied without batting an eyelid.

That was just the ticket, but I suggested to him maybe we should go back to my house, (after all, although he didn't know it, everything I needed was there). He agreed and we called a taxi, (I could have just asked the one I had arrived to wait, had I known).

When I opened the front door I didn't bother suggesting he sit in a chair in the lounge. We were both adults and we both knew why he was here, so I couldn't see the point in pretending. I went straight to the kitchen and got a bottle of Vodka from the freezer, collected two glasses along the way, and led him into the bedroom – which I had tidied before going out – hoping for just this situation. He paused in the doorway and I had a sinking feeling in my stomach, as I wondered if he was not as brave as he had appeared in the disco. It seemed I had judged him wrong, and I needn't have worried, because he soon entered the room, took me in his arms and the fun started.

It all happened the way I wanted; little of the hugging and kissing rubbish and straight into sex. He stripped, I stripped and we fell onto the bed already joined. At first he pumped away normally, but soon he rolled me over so I was astride him, and then he held me as I moved in circles, back and forth, up and down, and round in a hip swivelling motion. Oh what exquisite pleasure! He was big in every sense, both long and wide and settling down on him I could feel him go right into me. Heaven!

Soon he turned me again and teased me by pulling out and moving lightly at my opening, in and out, in and out, in … oh God this was good. Just as I was losing myself in what his big phallus was doing, he stopped.

"No you don't" he said.

I was impressed. He didn't know me and yet had realised I was working myself towards orgasm.

“Don’t worry. I am known for my multiple organisms”, I replied.

But still he waited, paused above me with his shaft just touching me, then with no warning he plunged in as deep as he could and pumped furiously. Soon we both climaxed and lay for a few minutes, then I got up and opened my cupboard. I brought out a beautiful lacquered black Chinese box with gold inlay, placed it beside him on the bed, and opened it. He looked inside and then looked at me quizzically.

“Take your pick”, was all I needed to say.

He chose two vibrators, not any two – but only after carefully weighing and measuring them. Then with my soft handcuffs he fastened my arms and legs to the bedposts, (I had chosen the bed purposely, although the salesman was only told I wanted one that was ‘sort of a four-poster but didn’t go right up to the roof’), and he stuck one large vibrator into my vagina and a smaller one up my anus. He set the small one to vibrate on slow/medium, and, finding some tape in my box of tricks, he taped it in place so it acted like a butt plug as well as a vibrator.

What he did with the other, was something I had always known existed but had never found. When I used these tools myself, I knew I was just missing vital areas, but couldn’t get anything positioned right while making sure the rabbit kept her ears on my clitoris, but he did manage it. After a while he removed the tape from the other machine and used the two at the same time. He moved them in and out simultaneously, then alternating, then moved them round and round and back and forth. My second orgasm was so much longer coming than the first, I was able to lie back and delight in this pleasure for ages before climaxing.

So many men wanted quick sex; jump on, bang about a bit and go home, and surprisingly few were comfortable with playing and experimenting – especially when it was the woman proposing the games. This was everything I had always dreamed of, even though I knew this thought was a bit of a cliché.

When my turn came to lead, I got a bottle of champagne I kept in the hope of trying something, and brought it back with an extra-large, tall glass. I suddenly wondered if his dick would fit inside the glass, as it really was big. It did, so I filled the glass with tepid champagne and gently placed his dick inside. He said the feeling was wonderful, partly tickly and partly pleasurable. I got him to hold the glass and I lay down, filling myself with bubbly pleasure, then told him to get inside me before all the bubbles popped. He didn't need told twice and afterwards we both agreed it was great. (I didn't tell him I had always wanted to try this, but had never found willing participants.)

Anyway, to cut a long night short, we experimented with all sorts of other things, and I decided I was in love – not with him, but with the sex. The good thing was that he agreed, and although neither of us normally chatted with our sex partners, we did that night.

We both loved sex, but mainly the experimenting and playing, and both of us had trouble finding partners to play with, so we agreed there and then to become 'Fuck partners', so either could call anytime and the other would come over to play.

Somehow it didn't ever get to that point as we spent all weekend in bed, and he never really left after that, but that suited too, as it meant 24 hour sex.

Between sexual escapades I found out his name was Ian Fielding and I told him mine was Katherine Kane. He asked if people called me Katherine or shortened it, and I said most just called me Kate. He felt that didn't suit me and either used my full name or called me Katie, which I liked.

He even looked good enough to be seen in public with too, which was a bonus. He was tall and had an athletic build, which looked to be due to sport, rather than hours in the gym; bright blue eyes and long, straight blond hair, (and I mean that really rich blond only nature can achieve). He had worn it in a ponytail when we met, but since then it had escaped and was loose. His clothes were subtle yet stood out, and they suited him. He had been wearing a pair of new looking straight legged jeans, an evening shirt, complete with cufflinks, (shot of course), and open at the neck, and a tan suede jacket which matched his tan Gucci loafers on his sock less feet. He was clean shaven and had no tattoos or piercing, so if I wanted, I could invite him to all the black tie dinners I had to attend, although that would imply a relationship we didn't have, but it was nice to have the option.

Another thing we talked about that night was work. He was a porn star, which worried me a bit because of STDs, but he assured me all participants were carefully vetted and healthy. He only did straight sex films because of his size, and also, he said, if you started deviating you were quickly expected to bang animals and anything else, and he wasn't into that.

I talked about my day and told him I might be unemployed by Monday – but he had an idea for my series… sex.

"Why not?" he queried when I hesitated. "Everything else has been turned into reality TV already, and there are loads of programs about sex on TV now. It isn't as far fetched as it may seem."

I saw his point, and started thinking about it.

"Not ordinary sex", he continued; suggesting we put people in a room and told them to be inventive. I then hit on the idea of providing various objects and toys they could use, to see what they chose and what they did with it. I also intended suggesting to my boss we needed to get any toys tested - to make sure they were safe, but in reality I wanted the chance to try them out at home.

Organising the Show

By the time Monday morning came I had it all thought out, the only thing missing was my boss, Mr Blyth's agreement. Mr Blyth had inherited a lot of money and with it seemed to come an equal amount of good luck. He had got to be head of television studios by chance more than ability, and that made him difficult to work for, as well as bitter – he knew the team that worked under his orders knew more than him, and he resented it – therefore we all paid the price.

He loved the new program idea and, I began to think he might be a closet pervert, as he wanted to sit in on the selection process – for the first time in the three years I had worked there. I thought I would keep an eye to see if my boss got excited at any point, as that should make him more manageable, and I could use that time to get him to approve ideas easier. He tended to deliberate for so long that ideas became old, or a competitor beat us to it, then he shouted at the team for not doing whatever it was earlier.

Apparently time was tight for getting it rolling, (I presume he had sat on the request for a new show so long it left me with no time to organise), so I was taken off the long-running house re-vamp series we were currently running, and told to get this moving 'ASAP'.

I set off with a big budget to buy lots of different sex toys for the show. We needed to know what each toy did, because the legal team wanted us to ensure that nothing we supplied was dangerous – so if anything happened, it was not our fault. I had told my boss I would find porn stars to use these and explain their functions, (I was hardly likely to tell him I had every intention of enjoying them to the fullest myself), and I would get a report on them.

It was great shopping with no limit, and when I got the toys home, Ian and I tried them all. Some were fun and some were boring, but at least we had new toys to amuse us for a couple of weeks. I had recommended Ian to my boss, (as an anonymous porn star), to run the auditions and be a judge on the show – for a healthy sum. Employing my own boyfriend wouldn't sound too good, so we had decided to keep that part of our relationship a secret – for now. Ian got to stop fucking, for the sake of it, (he had told me he had made a reasonable amount of money and now he only did it to be sure of a good shag, but now he had that with me – his words), and I got to keep my job because of Ian's idea for a show, so this seemed fair all round. As if that were not enough, we got all sorts of toys to play with, and hopefully a lot of new ideas for sexual games to try out at home.

Some of the toys were the run-of-the-mill vibrators, butt plugs, beads, eggs, bullets and so on for me; and for Ian there were cock rings, fleshlights and penis extenders, (Ian certainly did not need these), but there were also some that we weren't sure how to use or what to do with. Reading the instructions did take a bit of the pleasure out of these toys the first time round, but was necessary for the 'report' we had to hand over, but to be honest none of them seemed that great, except the vibrating rabbit cock ring which I enjoyed – more than once.

I spend my days organising rooms to hold auditions in, working with the lawyers to prepare contracts and a hundred other details to get ready to launch the show. Ian started coming into the studios every day to advice and help, and seeing him kept me on a constant high as my body started preparing for what the night ahead would hold. I stopped wearing knickers to work and gave up trousers. Under my, not too short, skirts I only wore stockings and a suspender belt, and Ian knew this and admitted he often felt a hard-on starting, at the thought of my wet pussy, there, ready for him, and he had to quickly find something to distract his senses and calm his dick.

We thought about the publicity announcing the show carefully, and decided to limit it to a few words:

"Do you like sex? Would you like to take part in a new TV show? Contact us by telephone or email at 0101002211 or newshowparticipate@Youcome.com for more information about auditions. Further details can be found on our website www.participatenewshow.com ".

The calls came in thick and fast, and the secretaries were kept busy taking all the details and sending audition applications. We had expected, (and hoped for), interest but as the concept was as yet untried, we were unsure about how many queries we could expect. So far things were looking good, but it was still early days.

It was a difficult and extremely busy time, trying to juggle so many balls and pick up objects at the same time, and a little glitch in our workplace made this harder. The glitch's name was Sarah. Our team was great and we often went out for drinks or dinner, and spent many pleasant evenings together. I wouldn't say we were all friends, but we got on fine and all tried to work together well, which made the job easier and more fun.

There were over thirty of us, between production and office staff, lightening and cameramen and a few others, and the only one who didn't get on well with anyone was 'Sour Pants' Sarah – a simple secretary. She acted as if she were in control, and kept telling people to do things that turned out to be wrong. She refused to do anything she was told and just did what she liked. She was nasty to everyone and made up tales to try and set some people against others. We all knew she intended to cause problems, and gave no credence to anything she said, but the constant back stabbing and complaining made everyone's life harder – to say nothing of having to re-do all her work and fix the mistakes she caused. As assistant producer, although I was actually running everything, I didn't have the power to fire her, or even send her to work in another place, where she could do less damage, and my boss didn't want to hear anything about this difficulty, so we had to put up with her.

Once all the preliminary stuff for the new show was in place, which took about three months, it was time to start the auditions. Ian had suggested this sort of thing might attract some weirdoes and so we organised a room a bit like a luxurious cell, where we could see into the audition room, but people in the room couldn't reach us, and the door to our sanctuary only opened when a code was punched in. We had a large shatterproof glass window and a speaker/intercom gadget so the participants could see and hear us, but could not reach us. We set up a big bed; large, soft rug; sofa and armchair, as well as a table and chairs in the audition room. There was a fridge full of odd bits and pieces; like bars of chocolate, fruit, drinks and so on, and a dresser with a red velvet cloth was covered with a wide assortment of sex toys; including empty champagne bottles and some of the lighter S&M paraphernalia. We had also put rings into the wall, a pole, a cage in the corner and a 'Joystick Vibrator Chair®*', (like a dentist's chair but with a big dick sticking up), and a whole host of other things – some obvious sex toys, others not, as that was what would make the program interesting – what the contestants choose and how they used it.

The participants were told it was a reality TV show just like the singing ones, but they would be judged on their sexual performance in different ways; how good they were – 2 points; their staying power – 2 points; how much they considered the other person – 3 points, (this made better TV), and their inventiveness – 3 points, (this was the really exciting part for Ian and I). Contestants with 5 points or more would be short listed, and from there, depending on how many good sexual couples we had, we would either further reduce the numbers, or they would all be on live TV.

We had told them to either bring a partner or wait in a room until another person who would make a single suitable partner, arrived, but we had set no limits otherwise, (provided they were coupled with another human; not a relation and over the age of consent), – gay was fine too and we got quite a few gay men, some alone and others already in couples, but only two couples of women. The rest were heterosexual and some looked really rough – but that was part of the game and the reason we stayed in our 'safe room'.

I had got one of the biggest sex toy companies to sponsor the show and they had provided a prize fund of half a million. This was to be shown in gold coins, (not real gold, but for show they certainly looked impressive), which we placed in a large, clear sphere with a hole in the middle where water, lit from within, spewed out like a rainbow and this 'gold fountain' stayed in full and tantalising view in the corner of the room. A large porn distribution company had said they would pay for any interesting clips from the auditions and live shows to make a compilation film, so all in all, quite lucrative for participants and the TV company alike, if enough participants were good enough to provide material to make a film.

I intended to ask my boss to give me a raise as a reward for all the additional money I was making for the company, and to compensate for the extra work and headaches this gave me, and if he refused I was toying with getting the sponsors to give me a percentage of sales from these extras, as the additional income for the TV company was rather large.

* *The 'Joystick Vibrator Chair®', is shaped like a reclining dentist's chair but with a moveable cock attachment, (that can be removed if you have guests you would prefer not to see what you enjoyed in your spare time). The shaft can be standing straight up so you sit on it, or lying at an angle so you can lie down, either forwards or backwards. There are two dildos as well, so you can fill each orifice.*

There are also bonds for your wrists and ankles. These can be manually closed and opened, or done by remote control. There is the choice of a small remote you hold in your hand, (strapped to your palm so it does not accidentally fall), or buttons on the ends of the arm rests. The left hand button closes the restraints and the right one opens them.

The chair also has a well-padded hole, so a man can put his penis into it. The gel-like substance underneath this, fits any size phallus and holds it tightly. There are attachments available to buy as extras, which include a masturbation ring, (a small, soft ring that moves up and down on a rubber shaft. The base of this shaft can be held in place with the user's bum - coming up through his legs, or be attached to the chair), and there is also a 'pineapple'. This is a sophisticated sac-like attachment that is swung into place, and like the hole, is made of a soft, flexible gel to fit any male genital. It is self-lubricating, and I am told works on the same principle as the small fountains you can buy, where there is a continual flow. It also has a temperature control so you can set it to match the warm place a vagina is.

Ian and I had thought up this new idea for a sex toy and we had talked about it to John Browne, one of the major manufacturers in this field. He liked it very much, and the three of us had come to an arrangement – the sex toy maker would make a prototype, which Ian and I would 'get someone to try' so they could give feedback, then John would improve it until it worked perfectly. Once any glitches were ironed out John would make another, which would be launched during the show, and the whole chair would belong to the three of us. Ian knew a good lawyer who drew up a contract, dividing the proceeds equally, but also giving Ian and myself anonymity, (which we wanted), and giving John the credit for having thought of the contraption, (which he wanted). This made us all very happy, and I got to keep the first fully working chair as an added perk.

Auditions

In our little room were the sponsors and porn industry professionals who were backing the programme, as well as my boss, (allegedly all present to protect their interests, but I think they simply wanted to watch the show). There were also the three official judges, Ian, a somewhat famous ex-prostitute turned madam, called, of all things, Bertha, and a porn film director named Nigel, also two cameramen who had set up cameras in the audition room but needed to monitor them in case of malfunction, myself and Jessica, (an able office worker who often helped me). I would have a vote along with the judges, but not on the sex side of things, rather from the point of view of what might appeal to the public or what would repel them. I had 2 points I could add or subtract from any couple if I wished, and this generally was enough to change their status from pass to fail and vice versa.

Unknown to anyone, Ian and I had sorted out our own code; left side meant, 'I don't like this' and right side, 'I do and want to try it at home – so pay attention'. We had practiced this at home to make sure we got it right and did not spontaneously use the wrong side. Our signs were anything from touching an arm or leg, to looking over that shoulder or standing on that side. This wasn't really necessary, but it did let each of us know what the other wanted to do that evening and raised our already high sexual tension.

People had been wandering into the room all morning, to see if we wanted coffee, tea, water, anything at all, and knowing this was an excuse to peek at the coupling happening on the other side of the window, rather than a genuine interest in our welfare, I nominated one person to fetch and carry food and made it a 'closed room'; no one else to enter. It wasn't that big and there was little point in all of us professionals being squashed to one side, with poor vision of what was taking place, so others could have their jollies.

We had done a lot of reality TV series, but these were either done using a format of existing shows we bought from other countries, or existing shows we changed enough to make our own. Either way we had a good idea of what would work, what wouldn't, and what problems to expect. This programme was so new I knew there would be pitfalls I hadn't foreseen and things that would need changed as we went along, so the first day was very much an anxiety laden, trial run, with me paying close attention to every aspect.

The first applicants had come as a couple and were unpleasant to look at, even fully clothed. He was tall and lanky and looked about twelve, with a face full of pimples; she was short and a ball of lard of indeterminate age, but definitely old enough to be his mother – so we checked, (just in case), but she wasn't. They would have to do something extraordinary to make it worthwhile having them on the show, because they really were repulsive.

Unfortunately, or perhaps fortunately, they were no good. She lay like a lump of meat and his thin spiky bun went up and down for ages before she yelled like a stuck pig and they both grinned. This prompted me to make a note that we needed to set up a room with a cold shower and bed, outside this area, so we can stop any really bad ones before they are finished and send them there, if they wished to continue. It didn't seem right to stop a couple mid-sex, leaving them with actual physical pains due to unreleased passion, but otherwise this process would take too long to get through, and the couples could use the shower, or bed, in that room if they wish to achieve satisfaction, but without wasting our studio time.

The next few pairs to audition were better, but conventional, and as the day wore on with nothing new, interesting or different, I was beginning to see my programme go down in a ball of flames before it started – but then, near the end of a very long day, we got our first participants to qualify for the next round.

They fitted everyone's bill – they were average build, plain and shy looking, but banged like it was going out of fashion – a good surprise for the audience. They both took the initiative, but the female slightly more often – again a bit more unusual, and they both examined the table carefully before starting. They picked up a butt plug each and some other stuff that I couldn't see clearly from this angle, prompting another note to move the table of goodies so both us and the audience could see the selection. Their choice turned out to be; anal beads for both of them, a G-spot vibrator for her and a cock ring for him. Granted these toys are not terribly inventive, but considering these people were being watched and filmed for the first time, we all felt they put on a good show and fucked like the end of the world was near. They scored a rating of 7 with the judges, so were through to the next part.

The auditions continued, and like any reality TV show we got a mix of contestants, although average people who were fine, but not memorable, were in the majority on our show. Several were boring, a few were just plain bad and then the disappointingly few who stood out for one reason or another. Basically it shaped up like any other reality TV audition, but our majority were forgettable, and that meant searching disparately through the tapes to try and fill the time slots for the audition shows.

I have to say I had hoped for better sex and some inspiration from our contestants, but most of them were less adventurous than me and we saw little action that we wanted to try at home. It was mostly her on top, him on top, her legs round her head, bent over a chair, from behind – all the things average people do every day, and a bit disappointing on the whole. One thing I noticed was that there was little breast and nipple touching with the participants going mainly for the genitals. I would have a word with the finalists before the live shows and suggest they include boobs in their routine in some way.

Another surprise was underwear – it was normally the sort of stuff you could buy in any shop, not sexy, silky or even rude, and here too I wanted to get some of the contestants wearing special, sexy sets. Two of the women did not even wear matching pants and bra, and one man had Y-fronts! These items would have to disappear. This was another potential sponsor I had overlooked, and resolved to contact one of the major manufactures about providing free undies in return for the publicity. This would get two birds with the one stone, the participants would be wearing nice looking underwear and we would get more sponsors and publicity, companies advertised 'As seen on ..'

I had had expectations of getting three or four shows out of the audition tapes, but more than two was not looking likely at this stage, as there was so little of note. I had initially thought that if we had more passes than we used, we could ask some of them if they would like to be part of audition tapes by doing it again, and this time we would give them a push in a more interesting direction. However so far we were struggling to find enough couples for the show, never mind any extra. Bad ones, who believed they were the best and sexiest people on earth, abounded, but generally there was nothing funny or interesting in their lack of skill, and this made unexciting viewing – but a few did stand out.

One couple did make us laugh and everyone present was in stitches, holding their stomachs with tears running down their cheeks. One man called his male partner 'my little brussel sprout' and in return he was referred to as 'my cherry tomato'. They had names for everything and 'carrot stick' was either cock or dildo – we were laughing too much to figure out exactly which, butt plugs were sweet peas, a rabbit vibrator was a 'dog's tongue', anal beads seemed to be 'green beans', handcuffs were 'chilli' and something else was 'garlic'. Quite where these names came from we couldn't figure out, but the whole performance gave us such pleasure we had already decided they would be great on the show – until, unfortunately, one of them got cold feet, so to speak. Actually he got limp dick half way through, which he was unable to overcome, and although that did not mean the end in theory – he could have used his mouth or hands on his partner – he then dissolved into floods of tears, and his partner spent a long time consoling him. No show for them, but we would include the funny names part in the audition tapes show, leaving out the sad failing of his body parts, to save him too much humiliation.

Then there was the Italian Stallion from Birmingham: a shiny, orange coloured man, with gelled back 1970's hair and pieces of facial hair that looked more like a part he had missed when shaving, than a designer beard. His appearance was enough to make him stand out as being hilarious, although from the way he strutted, that was not the effect he was going for. He came with a frumpy, mousy wife, which made us speculate on the possibility he had married her before he decided to become an orange Italian sex symbol. As we all predicted, the sex didn't last long and wasn't great – she lay down, he rammed in and out and climaxed, end of session. What was great was his other performance. He was proud of his cock and showed it off to the camera, even going towards one for a close up. The dick in question was a reasonable width and seemed quite long; although it was so bent it was difficult to tell. (I wanted to find out if a dildo existed that was shaped like this because it was stimulating me a lot imagining it inside me, (although not attached to that idiot), because I could imagine it hitting my G-spot like little else.)

We got many odd scenes and a few sad ones. Then there were the sickening ones where one partner felt they had to humiliate the other. The worst of these were a couple in their fifties. She started belittling him from the minute they walked into the room and didn't stop the whole time. It quickly became obvious he didn't want to be there, and had only agreed to keep his wife happy, so to speak, as happy is not a word suited to that harridan. Everything he did was wrong, "as usual", she hated him, everyone hated him, their friends loathed him but put up with him as they liked her so much, and on and on it went. All of us in the room felt terribly sorry for him and it was obvious that after years of this browbeating, he had come to believe he was worthless. This was one result I wanted to give personally, so I left the room to deliver the news.

Looking at the wife I said, "I am sorry, but, although we would have taken you, based on your husband's performance, (not true but I felt so sorry for him), we couldn't stand you because you are such a nasty bitch and the general public would vote you off straight away. No one in the whole world could ever find you likeable, (one of her pet phrases to him), and none of us here ever want to see such a nasty piece of work again."

It had occurred to me half way through my tirade that she may take this disappointing news out on him, which was the opposite of my intention, but this notion came too late. When I had finished I noticed, with relief, he was standing taller and straighter. I had managed to give him back some dignity after all. She opened her mouth and he interrupted, "Not now my dear. Time to go home" and grabbing her arm pulled her out the door.

When I walked back into the room there was a big cheer, and I felt great to have helped, at least I hoped I had.

Then there were the ones that were very inventive, albeit a bit frenzied, such as the lady who stuck two fingers up the man's anus and tickled his cock with a feather, all at the same time. Her partner then stuck both his dick and a small magic wand vibrator into the woman, (that opened all our eyes and was one of the few times I touched Ian's right side indicating I wanted to try it that night – and although it was tight at first, it was worth it!) This pair seemed to feel obliged to use every piece of equipment on the table and provided us with enough audition tape to make up for some of the boring ones, so things were looking up a bit.

There was a couple that divided opinion and left me with a dilemma. The man entered the room naked and the woman was fully clothed. That intrigued us to begin with. When he spoke, he had the most incredible voice. Soft yet strong, cultured and so very, very sexy it was unbelievable. He was also French, with just the right amount of accent to get women wet whatever he said.

He began, "Imagine you are in the Caribbean and on a private beach." She started to remove her clothes in a sexy way that was not a striptease, but even more inviting.

When she was naked he continued, "You want to lie down and get some sun before having a swim, so spread your towel and lie down." She took a clean towel from the table and spread it on the floor. Gracefully she lowered herself onto it and lay relaxed, but with her lags closed.

"You can hear the water and the waves lapping on the sand. Whoosh, whoosh, whoosh. You do not open your eyes but somehow know the waves are getting closer. You feel them tickle your feet and the water is warm and pleasant."

Not a sound happened in our room and everyone was hypnotised by his voice and words.

"Now you feel it creeping up your legs and you want to feel it inside you." She opened her legs.

"It has reached your most intimate parts and is invading your body. The feeling is wonderful." She started arching her back and moaning gently.

He continued until, without touching her in any way, he brought her to orgasm, and if truth be told many of us observers were not far away either. I don't know if it was his voice or the concept of the waves or a combination of both, but it was seriously powerful stuff.

We all agreed this had to be part of our show before realising it was not over.

"You have had enough sun and wish to go home now", he continued.

She got up and started to get dressed. First a small delicate, white tango slid up her legs, and then as she bent to pick up her bra, the man rushed over and said in a totally different tone, "Where do you think you are going, bitch? You are asking for it. I know you want it," and quickly ripping off her tango proceeded to mock rape her. I say mock, as she insisted afterwards that she knew what he intended to do, but for all the world it looked like a real rape.

Even after they left the room we were all rooted to the same spot we had been in, and no one spoke for ages.

I struggled to get control of myself and said, "Right, how about them then?"

"Wow! Em... OK, well... I don't know," was the first answer from Bertha.

"Yes, definitely. Great TV", the porn director exclaimed.

Opinion in the room was divided. Some thought we should keep them but only doing the first part, others thought the shock of the 'rape' was good for the show and others believed it all too weird and better left out.

I sent someone to tell them we were still thinking and called a break. I took the judges, Jessica and a cameraman, who had already offered some good insightful thinking, for a cup of coffee and a chat away from the set. We talked for quite a time and finally I decided to let the whole performance be part of the show. The public could decide to keep them or send them home and would certainly remember that episode, just like we would.

I had set the live TV show up, so that the first three quarters was contestants doing their thing, followed by voting for ten minutes, during which we would show the more interesting auditions, followed by the results. This was one audition we would not include, either on the audition shows or during the final, at least, not until after they had performed this routine again, as I wanted the shock factor to be part of their performance.

There was also my bête noir; a stunning looking blonde woman who was so sensual we were all wet just looking at her walk into the room. She oozed sex with every graceful movement, and every person in our room was transfixed. She slowly removed her cloths and by the time she was finished, judging by the quite groan, someone behind me had anticipated the rest of her performance. Then she draped herself on the bed and a naked man appeared beside her. He must have come in with her, but not one person had noticed him. He lay down prone and she proceeded to dedicate her hands to herself and him, alternatively and together, until their climaxes happened simultaneously, (and from the dash to the bathrooms afterwards, the climaxes in the other room were not the only ones). Ian, Nigel and I were left alone, and my heart sank when Ian put his hand on my right arm. There was no way I could reproduce anything like that at home, and knowing I would fall so short of this spectacular display, I knew I would feel silly trying. (I got off that embarrassing failure as Ian said he didn't want to offend me but he didn't expect me to reproduce that exactly, but just wanted us to do it in that way - where he did nothing and I did it all – whew! That was a relief.)

Neither Ian or Nigel were terrible impressed with the act, as both said she was so wrapped up in herself, the man was merely a prop and technically there had been no sex, as it was all hand jobs, but every other person present agreed we needed her, and by association him, on the show, to add another touch, so to speak. Then we later discovered an extremely interesting fact about them during the live final, which added an element of naughtiness to the whole act.

On the whole Ian, Nigel and I agreed on the contestant's abilities, or lack of, while Bertha went for some off the wall choices. She loved two lesbians who both insisted on strapping dildos to themselves. They were somewhat inventive apart from that, and Ian and Nigel gave them a passable rating. I just found it weird and not interesting, (one with a dildo I could see, but not both), however, as a novelty factor they would suit fine, and the public could vote for them to stay or leave depending if they agreed with

Bertha or I, so I chose to leave them in the show for now as a sort of wild-card – to use if we needed to make up numbers – (luckily we didn't, but it added to the length of the audition tapes which was now just about enough long enough to fill three shows).

We got a few who came as threesomes, but unfortunately these were always two girls and one man, and all they did was have straight sex with the two men filing the woman's front and back openings. There were no groups with two men, but in one of the threesomes, a man had appealed to us all. He made many suggestions for using the props provided, but these were quickly rejected by the woman, who wanted straight sex. Having discussed this with the others, I sent Jessica to chat to the man, to find out if he was the female's boyfriend. When she reported that he was, but they were fighting, I went out and got him into a room alone with me, where I suggested he might like to join another couple as a second man. He jumped at this chance, and it was obvious his desire to be on TV was more important than his relationship.

The woman said if he did the competition without her, they were through, and he simply said, 'Fine'. We just needed a couple to work with him, but when the auditions were through, we could look back to find an average pair and offer them the chance of being included if they accepted him into their act. As it turned out there were none suitable, but there was a single gay man who needed a partner, and the two of them agreed to make up a couple, which was just as well for us, as they ended up being our only gay participants, even though we had hoped to cater to a wide range of tastes.

We had a few scary moments, and one close call with death. At the point of orgasm, one man went into an erotic asphyxiation routine. His girlfriend climaxed, and it was major, but when he too climaxed, it went on and on. With his hands still round her neck, she started to turn a funny colour. The medics rushed in and pulled him off, but at first she didn't seem to be breathing. Luckily they were able to bring her round, unharmed, but undaunted, she did want to 'try again immediately it was so good'. We sent them home and were all a bit taken aback. If they continued doing this, we felt she would die, but they were both adults, and there was little we could do except warn their doctor, (getting the doctor's name was part of the application process), and not show their video, in case it inspired others to try the same thing.

Another near tragedy happened, when during intercourse the woman apparently did not show enough enthusiasm, and the man started to thump her, and I do mean thump. He broke her nose, a couple of ribs, gave her a black eye and lots of cuts before the guards managed to get him off. She didn't want to press charges as 'he didn't mean it', and we gathered this was neither the first time nor would it be the last. Again a call to her doctor, and a ban from our show, were all we could do, because, although a few of the people present tried to talk to her, she wasn't interested in hearing what we had to say.

There were also a couple of drugs brought in without our knowledge, one amyl nitrate and two cocaine users were summarily removed, and their products thrown away. The part of this I didn't understand was where they got the money to buy these drugs, as the couples involved were, in their own words, 'poor', and this paraphernalia is not cheap, but I suppose the saying, "where there is a will, there is a way" is true.

On more than one occasion when the pair were thanked and told they would not be going through, one or both of them turned nasty. We got a lot of verbal abuse and one couple threw anything and everything they could find at the window when they were told they were going home.

I had got a couple of bouncers to be ready, on hand if they were needed, and while they were able and willing to deal with the men, the women caused them a few moments concern. My bouncers did not want to be too rough with a 'lady', no matter what I said, but when one such female seriously hurt a cameraman, who was sorting out a problem with the camera, by bashing his head against his tripod and breaking his nose, the bouncers finally stepped in and did their thing. The woman was literally thrown out of the building, and the poor cameraman, who insisted he was fine, was taken to hospital for a check-up. Apart from his broken nose, there was no damage, and he insisted on returning to work the next day with black eyes and a swollen lip.

I spoke to Mr Blythe about this incident and suggested we offer Sam, the poor punch bag, a paid holiday somewhere nice, for him and his wife, when the show was over. The boss was not keen at first, but seeing this might avoid a serious 'personal injury caused in the workplace' law suit, he eventually agreed. I believed Sam wouldn't have sued us, but the unions might. Sam was delighted with his compensation and told the union he was not prepared to do anything and to leave it alone, as he was happy.

There was a couple who were causing us some problems about whether to include them or not. They were good, inventive and appealing, but the sex lasted ages. They would both build up to a climax and then do something else to stop it coming, then start building up again. This worked well, as when it did come, their orgasms were spectacular. The problem was, the 'something else' was not terrible arousing to watch, as it had to be not too stimulating for them. Most of what they did was great, but we couldn't expect the public to watch them for fifteen or twenty minutes when not much was happening. If the shows hadn't been live, we could simply have done an edit and removed the duller moments, but as it would be live, that wasn't possible. I asked Jessica to have a chat with them to see if they could speed it up a bit, and they agreed to try, but when they came back the next day, it was longer than before and took a total of thirty five minutes. That was fine for real life, but not our show – for many reasons, one being there would be little time left for other contestants, but also we would lose the viewer's interest. With regret we had to tell them they could not participate, but Ian and I played that game all night to great avail.

One day while Ian and I were talking about that day's contestants, Ian made the remark that one of the men should just have 'stayed home to wank' and that sparked an idea. Next year we could include masturbating championships for both men and women, either during the show, or as a spin off series – and spin offs were something TV companies loved. That should hopefully gain me more points towards a raise, and I had some more ideas of topics that may suit too, such as; a reality TV show for most perverted; a man with a permanent hard on and women trying to make him come – the same with a frigid woman.

The Villa

At first I had to run every move I made past my boss, but as time wore on he let me make more and more decisions alone and I only went to him when large sums of money or serious filming difficulties were involved. One instance of this was when I discovered there was nowhere to place the table of toys, to have it fully in view without it blocking some important area, and that meant we needed another camera and cameraman.

Another such occasion was where the live final was to be filmed. Our idea, (Ian's and mine, that is), was to get the couples together in a house and film them twenty-four hours a day. Legally they had to be told they were being filmed, but after a day, or two at most, we believed they would forget about the cameras and we might get sex in some weird places and kinky ways – and record some great TV. I had the idea of trying to get a large mansion on a small, deserted, tropical island. Providing there was no one else in the area, we could set up cameras all around the island and have small boats or canoes on the beach, (we would remove the paddles so the contestants didn't get out of camera reach). Sand, surf, sun and palm trees should produce some coupling, but we couldn't offend holiday makers by letting it happen on a public beach.

It would be interesting to see if any couples swapped or got together to practice with each other, and what rooms they used. It would also let the audience get to know the people involved better, as they would be seen eating, talking, doing whatever hobbies they have, and, as villas like this always have a pool, the participants might skinny dip. As my boss seems to be enjoying the auditions rather a lot, I hoped he may agree to this expense if he thought he could watch orgies, so I reminded myself to push this possibility when talking to him about the house.

As I was thinking about this villa and what could happen there, I hit on another bright idea – genitalia food! I know the Italians make penis shaped pasta, as I had seen it while on holiday there, and had even brought a packet home for fun, so dear knows what other food stuff comes in erotic shapes. I may even manage to get the food producing companies to supply it free, in return for the good publicity they would get, and this should impress the boss.

We could also get a baker to make penis shaped bread that had an aphrodisiac in it – anything to make them hornier. Even some substance that made them loose their inhibitions baked into the bread would be great, if there is a legal one. A random fact intruded at this point; walnuts, (I think it is walnuts but it might be Brazil Nuts, so must check), can be sexually transmitted, so we need to be careful to find out if any contestants are allergic to nuts, and if so, ensure there are no walnuts in the food.

I brought up the villa idea, but it was instantly shot down, (Blyth hadn't even asked the cost), as too expensive, and I was told to 'find something in town'. The problem was, that was not easy, at least not to find a house that was potentially interesting and big enough. We needed something more than the normal rooms, a Jacuzzi at least, or a sauna, maybe a games room and pool table, after all, strip billiards, (maybe it was pool or snooker – something with those big, green tables anyway), had become popular recently after featuring in the news. We could have a nude picnic and see if anything interesting happened there too – really, with a self-contained house like the villa, the sky was the limit, but for now something like that was forbidden to me.

After a lot of searching I had a few possibilities, but none of them really satisfied me. I had, however, found the perfect island mansion in the Caribbean, having not given up my idea at the first “no”. It belonged to Samantha Sighn, (aptly enough pronounced ‘sigh’), an aging, out-of-work film star who had fallen on hard times, but was reluctant to sell. She would let us rent it for a reasonable sum as long as she could play hostess. This was the part I wasn't sure about – her name would get us some extra publicity and viewers, but what could she do, and would she get in the way? She lived there and claimed she had nowhere else to go, and I felt a presence like Samantha's might inhibit things a little for our couples.

This house was a vital part of the show, and it was starting to worry me I hadn't got anything settled yet, but short of keeping looking with my fingers crossed, I wasn't sure what to do. Another worry was that no one had managed to come up with a good enough name for the show and we needed that soon to do some marketing and promotions.

During the auditions Ian and I had started to spend more time together publicly and even started leaving and arriving together. When, as we had known would happen, someone asked me if we were seeing each other, I said we were. We had planned it this way because it wouldn't have looked good me giving my boyfriend a part in the show, but as long as no one knew the real order of our getting together, this was perfectly acceptable.

It was official; Katherine was screwing the porn star! We were happy it was no longer a secret and as Ian fitted into the band of workers well, everyone was happy for me and included Ian in any work outings. He endeared himself to everyone with his easy manner and willingness to help. On more than one occasion he had dashed over to help lift or move heavy objects, had comforted one of the make-up ladies when she found 'too many penises' a bit daunting, and was present and involved more than the other judges. In production meetings where he was present, he was diplomatic about getting any idea passes and generally, well… perfect really.

Promotion

My boss had me doing much more on this show than my job description demanded, and more than I usually did, therefore I was determined to get some form of acknowledgement for all my hard work, to say nothing of the hours I was putting into this production and the stress levels which were reaching mega proportions. That is why, when I hit upon another masterful idea, I decided to try a spot of coercion.

I asked for a meeting after auditions one day. I knew watching people 'going at it', as he liked to say, put him in a receptive mood, proved by the fact that when he called me in, he offered me a whisky. Good sign. This was normally a treat reserved for senior colleagues and clients. His, "call me Simon" that followed however, was totally unexpected.

I told him I had had wonderful ideas for free publicity, but did not have the clout to carry them through. I added I also felt drained by running the whole thing and thought I should step back a bit. I was really doing his job as well as my own; I should have been overseeing and not managing *and* overseeing. I explained that not having sufficient power made life too hard.

"I am assistant to the producer, and no one wanted to take orders from an assistant. People want to talk to the boss and not his lackey; meaning decisions are questioned and things are just not getting done. I wondered if you could take the reins back, as the cameramen are threatening to strike, because they are working extra hours, the makeup girls are being squeamish about the amount of flesh they see every day. Only you have the clout to deal with this, offering a compromise or threat. I am also getting anonymous threatening letters from prudes who have heard rumours about the content in our show, and begging letters from others who want to watch the auditions for a weird variety of so called "valid" reasons."

All this was true, and there was even more of it, but I was enjoying having so much control, and thrived on pressure. Having Ian in my life helped, and back home, a really good fuck released all the days' annoyances and left me feeling relaxed and satisfied. Another good thing about Ian being in my house was that we could talk about the show, and he was as passionate and involved in it as me, so discussions were long and fruitful.

In the evenings we had our own sex games and these depended on our mood, how much energy we had left after the day's shooting, and what time it was. Coming home at 1.30 am when you have not eaten, and knew you had to get up at 7.00 am for another long day, was not conducive to long and inventive sex, and those evenings we usually had plain sex – in bed – good, but not as much fun as other, more involved types.

When we felt inclined, this changed and we experimented; sometimes we dressed up – he as 'the masked man who enslaved and ravished me', or me as 'a maid with a short skirt and no knickers and a penchant for dropping things'. We tried a rape scene, and while I enjoyed it, I did find it hard to struggle to escape when all I wanted was to grab his cock and shove it inside myself as quickly as possible.

Other evenings we did so much foreplay there was actually little sex. We used vibrators, toys, hands, mouth, feathers, hair and anything else we could find. My favourite scene was one of us tied to the four bed posts with tissue paper. The rules were you could not break the paper, and as it was so fragile the slightest movement ripped it, so you had to stay totally still while the other person did everything they possibly could to stimulate you to the point of moving. I don't know if concentrating so hard on not moving was responsible, but we both achieved massive orgasms when playing this one. Strange really when both of us tried to stimulate by touching breasts, nipples, thighs and feet, in short, anything apart from the genital area. I supposed it must be that, the more the build up, the bigger the climax, but verifying this discovery would have to wait until work settled down, before there was time to do proper research.

However, back in the reality of work and drudge of life, I needed a promotion to make my voice heard, and money to make me happier with the incredibly long days, so here I was, listing all the things that needed fixed before I could even consider working on the free publicity, in the hope of either a new title or a raise or, better yet, both.

Simon did not want to do any of this work, as he could imagine his days spent watching the auditions going down the drain. I encouraged this idea, even though it was not necessarily correct, and most things could be managed from the audition room – that was what I did after all.

"Simon, people just won't listen to me", I tried again. "What! The *assistant* says we need to move or do it? What does the boss say? is all I get all day long, and I am spending so long trying to get people to take me seriously I have no time for anything else, and that is one reason I need you to step in."

"Well, that is easily resolved", he answered smugly. "I suppose I could become executive producer and you could be made producer. This was something I have been thinking about for a while anyway. I was just waiting until this show was in the bag before telling you."

(No you weren't! You were worried you would have no valid reason for watching the auditions, I thought, nastily but accurately.)

"That certainly would help with a lot of the difficulties", I answered, but prudently added, "but would you still be able to help with the auditions?"

"If you wished, we could make the announcement public, but in private you and I could agree that things will continue as they are, until this show is finished. That way I will be able to help you more."

"That sounds perfect", I quickly jumped in, failing to mention he had not uttered one word of help about the auditions so far.

"All right, I will tell everyone tomorrow morning, so you can now consider yourself producer."

One down, one to go.

"Er, Simon, I hate to be mercenary, but does the new title by any chance have a better salary? I only ask because finishing late every night and coming in early every morning means I am having to spend a lot on eating out, where normally I eat at home, to save money to pay the mortgage. I worry a lot about not being able to meet the payments and losing my house."

"We can't have you worried my dear child," (where had that come from – 'my dear child!').

"As producer you will be earning double your current salary, so at least I can lift that weight from your pretty little shoulders."

Was he hitting on me? 'Pretty little shoulders!' Choosing to ignore the odd phrases in the message, I concentrated on the main event – more money – and thanked him profusely.

Just in case he was trying it on, I launched into my publicity ideas before the situation became awkward.

"We could set up Facebook, Twitter and You Tube accounts for the show and people could comment, vote and post their own videos. We could run a side-by-side social media competition where users send their home videos and readers vote for the best ones. I could try to get some good prizes, such as a free holiday, concert tickets for a year and other things I haven't yet thought of, as well as sex toys from our sponsors, of course, for any film that stood out. The online competition could have a few levels; video and written. The written one would be the most provocative description or story, or a running commentary on Twitter."

I knew Simon would take all this to the head of programming as if it were all his own invention, making himself look good, but I had got what I came for, and that suited me fine.

One time a few nights ago, while Ian and I had been chatting about the show in bed, we had talked about connecting it to a web site and to a video phone site. Ian suggested he and I buy these two sites and let the show use them, (after all the TV company did not want to be bothered running these after the show finished, but it would give us a reasonable income.) Ian was good on computers and his friend, Jack, who had got him into porn films, was apparently a computer whizz. Jack could maintain these and do the technical stuff and Ian could run them, then if I left my job for any reason, (including being fired for having too much power, another hang up of Simon's), I could work on them too. Jack would get 30% of each site and Ian and I, 35% each. It sounded good, but like the sex toy chair –my ownership had to stay secret.

Jack had found a failing VoIP business and bought it for the proverbial song, and before long it was all set up and running – it just lacked customers. We renamed this service 'SCall' and it was to work the same way as any VoIP, but people used their web cams for sex, either alone, or group sex, online.

One day I suggested to my boss that we should use a website and VoIP where users could get involved, again sending videos and stories, adding that Ian owned one of each already and I thought he would let us use them. The site had a great name; theshagger.com and the VoIP was SCall, (S for sex). Simon loved the idea and the names and told me to organise it.

All this info had the desired effect and I was no longer his 'dear child'. He loved every single idea, so within the space of half an hour I had got a promotion and a raise, earned a lot for a site and hopefully the webcam service, and given myself a few months' work to be completed within a few days. As I was thinking this, another thought struck me – I could do with an assistant, but there was no way I could bring that up now, not after haggling for two major changes already.

I must have sighed, as Simon asked what was wrong.

"I was just thinking about fitting this all into tomorrow," I replied.

"You need an assistant", he said much to my surprise.

"That would certainly make things easier."

"What about Sarah?" he mentioned one of the people who worked under me, (the one we called 'Sour Pants').

"I don't like Sarah, and more importantly neither does anyone else. In fact everybody hates her and does everything possible to avoid her. No one would take orders from her and we would have a rebellion," I replied honestly, looking at my hands in embarrassment as I delivered this tirade. "Jessica is very competent and well respected, is there any chance she could do it?", and with that I looked up.

Too late I realised he and Sarah were having an affair. His face had 'wounded lover' written all over it.

Working on a television show requires quick and effective thinking on your feet, so I tried some of that to remedy the situation.

"The problem with Sarah is, women hate her because she is prettier and they are jealous – and we all know that leads to untold and insurmountable difficulties. Men ask her out and she refuses, so they hate her too, either so they can protect their manhood by saying they don't want her, or because by refusing them they feel rejected and resentful. Girls like Sarah will always have trouble working with others for these reasons, and will not fit into any team or become friends with any other members of the team. I tried to persuade her to come out with the guys a few times when we were all going for a celebratory drink or dinner, but she always refused. She knows what people feel, and is not comfortable with it." (This was true up to a point. I had asked her, but her words were, 'I do not want to socialise with these losers,' and this attitude was the reason she was so loathed – along with being a pea brained, lazy tart.)

"I feel sorry for her, but she will never fit in here, and once already when she tried to be helpful and asked someone to do something – do you remember the lighting men's dustup – that was the outcome", I continued with crossed fingers.

Simon did remember. The lightening men had resented Sarah demanding they change the bulbs because she said they were unsuitable, when actually they were the very best, most suitable and most expensive around. Sarah had hounded them and not let them get on with their work, so they had all stopped work, taken out the offending bulbs, which cost nearly as much as a car, and had thrown them onto the floor. This had effectively stopped work until replacement bulbs could be found, and had cost the company thousands and thousands, while everyone hung around waiting until replacement bulbs were located. It also caused rather a lot of embarrassment, especially as it delayed an advert of a major sponsor.

"The lightening people are against her for that incident, the cameramen took their colleagues side and are also against her, and those are two large and powerful groups of workers," I continued.

"Yes, but if she were boss they would just have to do as she said," he said in a tone I knew all too well meant 'I have decided'. I would have to try a different tack quickly.

"She has just alienated the only person in the whole crew, who could have been on her side, Tommy from makeup, was her boyfriend until she started harassing one of the judges, Ian." I was watching his face closely and this seemed to be working – as long as he didn't shoot the messenger.

"The harassment became so bad, Ian asked me to make her stop, but she left a photo of her vajazzle on his desk with 'come into my world' written on it. She was wearing the vajazzle at the time, and none of us knew she had one, until one of the cleaners found the picture and showed it around. Tommy was furious and is now her number one enemy."

"Is all this true?" he asked quietly, and I knew the moment of truth was here where one of us would be fired. I knew my boss well – that was the reason I had worked so hard at getting the web site name, game and the other bits under my own name – he was unpredictable and unfair. He had sacked one employee simply because they had said they didn't think a certain colour of brown suited the curtains in one of our productions, as it looked like dog dirt. Simon's wife had chosen the curtains, and Simon's own boss had forced him to change the colour as it was wrong, but the employee was not re-instated.

I said hesitantly, "Yes, I have the offending photo myself, as the judge only asked me this afternoon to speak to Sarah and I haven't had time yet."

"Give it to me and ask her to come in" he barked.

I did as I was bid, and nervous, pretended to work until she came out, furious, and within five seconds had cleared her desk and left with not a word to anyone.

“Kate!” Simon bellowed.

I went in, heart thudding.

“Sarah has left. I will not have my employees behaving that way. If you think Jessica will do the job well, give it to her – but her work will be your responsibility. Oh, and find someone to take Sarah’s place – quickly, he added as an afterthought.”

I left him, thankful to still have my job, which I loved, happy about my promotion, but most of all delighted the only fly in the ointment had gone. We were a happy team and got on well on the whole. Sarah had spied on us and generally made things as difficult as possible, so we would all work even better with her out of the way.

A New Team Member

That evening, I recounted my interview with the boss to Ian, after we had both had a good go in *the* chair, as well as sex in the shower. The chair had become a habit after work, and we had decided we needed two, so we could use them together. It really was an amazing feeling to be tied there and have nothing to do except concentrate on pure pleasure. I had chosen a rabbit vibrator as an attachment, and knew just the setting I liked; strong thrusts and gentle caresses. Ian too knew what height and temperature he wanted the pineapple and ring, and we quickly settled down to gratification.

We both held out longer on our second orgasm, (as do most people), so having a quick bang on the chair was a release of the day's build up of sexual tension, so we could then start fresh with each other, and enjoy playing, slowly, taking time to dedicate to all sorts of foreplay.

Anyway, I had gone for a shower while Ian used the chair, but before long he had jumped in with me for another 'quickie', which turned into much more. We started in the shower, gently soaping each other all over, then continued by drying each other, and finally had a good long shag on the bathroom mat. By the time we got to bed, it started again when Ian touched my nipples so gently, as to leave me unsure if it was my imagination or not. When he started circling my dark circles, only occasionally and briefly flicking the sensitive peaks, I knew it was not wistful thinking, and lay quietly enjoying this form of teasing. He kneaded and sucked, until not only were my breasts taught and hard, but they felt as if they might explode. At that point Ian produced a vibrator from who knows where, inserted it, with both the pumping and rabbit ears on maximum, and placed his member between my swollen breasts. I felt the time had come to participate more fully, and held my breasts tight around his organ, while with incredible dexterity he moved the vibrator and his penis simultaneously until we both came with loud shouts.

When we finished that time, and were both lying spent, he said, “I don’t suppose you would consider my sister for the job? She is a secretary, receptionist and general dog’s body for a dental practice with five dentists, so knows how to juggle things.”

“You have a sister?” I questioned, surprised, as there had been no mention of any family at all.

“Yes, but I have never mentioned her as she has no idea what I do, or rather did, because I have always kept my work and private lives totally separate. Our parents died in an accident when I was seventeen and she was twelve. I was close to being eighteen at the time, and managed to stave off the authorities for a few months, then after my eighteenth birthday I got custody of her. I got a job in a grocer’s during the day, but there wasn’t enough money to keep her in school.”

“My father had made some bad investments and we were left in debt, with no other living family members to turn to for help. The house we were brought up in was quite big and I couldn’t afford to keep it. After it was sold – furnished – I managed to pay off all the debts and have enough to buy a very small apartment, but there was no money left for anything else – even furniture. I managed to buy Karen a bed, but at first I had to sleep on the floor. I only bought a second bed when Karen refused to use hers while I had none. I got to take home stale or old food from the grocer's and we lived on that, but there was never enough. I couldn't take on a second job as I needed to be there for Karen in the evenings."

"A guy I had been friends with had become a prostitute and was always asking me to join him, but it wasn't something I was comfortable with. When he got his first part in a porn film, and told me they wanted another male, I decided to try that. The money was very good, and I enjoyed the sex, so eventually I left my other job and only did films. Karen never knew – that is why I used a different surname, so word would not get back to her. She believed I had a job in films; without lying I managed to let her think my role was running errands and generally helping out. I earned a lot, and had lots of time to be with Karen, so it worked out well."

"Anyway, she hates her job, and one of the partners is always trying to corner her and touch her, and sometimes when he goes to conferences abroad he makes her go too. None of the others take her away overnight, so we both know it is not necessary. That is where she is now, in New York with him, but she gets back tomorrow. I would like you to meet her anyway."

"If she is suitable, and she may not be, no one must know of her relationship to you, as I would be accused of nepotism, and rightly so. If I do speak to her, but do not offer her the job, you must promise not to be angry with me." I wanted to make things clear as this seemed like a road full of land mines, but also could be an easy way of getting a replacement for Sarah.

"Yes. Great. No problem."

"Yes, there is a problem. Everyone at work knows you were a porn star. It might be time to tell her. You can tell her it was only for the money, and you have stopped, but I think she needs to know. Otherwise you need to keep away from here and make sure she doesn't watch the show."

"Good point, I hadn't thought of her finding out when the show aired. I am meeting her for lunch tomorrow, so I will tell her then. I hope she takes it well."

"You might also want to bring her back to see where you work, without mentioning the job, so she is not disappointed. We can meet in the foyer, and you can invent an excuse to leave. I will show her round and interview her at the same time, then, she will never know a job was available in case it doesn't work out."

That is what we did, and Karen was my saviour. It turns out New York had been a showdown and she was told, 'put out or get out', and she choose to leave. Unemployed and in a panic, she saw me as a saviour, not only of her, but also because I had rescued her brother from *that* job. She took Ian's past employment in her stride, and this cool attitude helped tip my decision to hire her. This job needed quick thinkers under pressure and there was no time to panic or faff about once recording started.

During production meetings I was generally very involved in the discussions, but Ian was present only to clear up any points that may arise. He passed the time by letting his fingers play with my vagina under the table. He played with my clit and then suddenly a finger penetrated, giving me that glorious 'filled' feeling that no one can adequately describe. Another finger would join the first and they turned and thrust. I marvelled at how no one noticed, and at how dexterous and inventive Ian was while not moving his upper body. I was also surprised I managed to make any sensible decisions while all this was going on. This was why I had stopped wearing trousers to work and only wore easily accessed skirts – it was too much fun to shut out, and had just the right element of danger that made it addictive.

"If your sister works with us, does that mean I will get no more hand jobs under the table?" I asked, worried.

"It won't make the slightest difference. No one must know anyway, so she will simply be another person who will remain in blissful ignorance of our pleasure", he reassured me.

Karen was quick, bright, got on with everyone and was totally and utterly dedicated to me and my welfare. She did everything she could to solve problems for me and even to keep them from reaching my ears. I very quickly made her my personal assistant, rather than production assistant, which I had already given to Jessica.

She even seemed to bring us good luck, as the auditions started taking a turn for the better. We had a higher calibre of sex happening, more interesting and inventive participants, and coupled with Sarah's departure, things started coming together so easily, I worried what was round the next corner.

Karen solved the villa problem in a simple manner. She had suggested asking the diva for photos of her home, and examining them showed us a gardener's cottage in the grounds. Karen suggested the diva move into the cottage for the duration of the shoot. That way she would be out of the action, and we could suggest to the lady herself, that this would be preferable for her. The actress could present the opening of each show, and conduct small interviews during the process. She could summon contestants to her cottage and grill them. That should appeal to her sense of self, and would let the general public get to know the people involved. I liked it a lot.

The diva agreed, reluctantly, but she had little choice except letting receivers enter her home instead of us. The next hurdle was my boss. Again, Karen stepped in, suggesting we find the ugliest and most boring, but most expensive houses in the local area and photograph them. Then we did boards with the photos and a list of facilities, along with price. I would take these to my boss, who hopefully would see the validity of the island paradise and acquiesce. If we chose carefully, we could make sure the villa was the most cheapest, but most attractive at the same time.

It all went just as Karen had said, and we had our finale setting. Now only more contestants and a name were missing to complete the pre-production part of the job.

A Name for the Show

Now I had more power to give orders and get people to listen to me, and with Jessica and Karen helping me out, I managed to get a bit more free time, which Ian and I enjoyed to the full. We left around dinner time and ate at home. We often cooked naked and sex happened more often than not during that chore, yet we still managed to get plates of properly cooked food onto the table, or wherever inspired us to consume it.

We usually walked or got the tube to work as it was easier than finding a parking space, but on the rare occasions we did take a car, we drove home with each trying to stimulate the other as much as possible. Ian's favourite trick was to take out his cock and gently rub it while watching me, stimulating me more than himself. When I was driving I was usually very wet and throbbing before parking at home and on more than one occasion I pulled into a dark area and we had quick sex there on the roadside. This offered temporary relief, but gear levers, steering wheels and too many clothes stopped either of us reaching the point of having enough. We had orgasms in the car, but these served only as appetisers so when we got inside the house frenzies of sex happened anywhere and everywhere, often just inside the door. On one occasion Ian had forgotten his key and mine had got lost somewhere in the depths of my handbag, as keys tend to do. As I was rummaging around looking for it Ian stood behind me and pulled my skirt up and I felt his dick nudge between my legs. Luckily, with high heels, I was just the right height for this act, and as I continued looking I bent forward slightly, opened my legs a bit and he stuck his penis in, encouraging me to keep trying to find the keys. He slowly went in and out, and although I kept looking in my bag, I couldn't see anything and could only feel his hard length moving deep inside me. I wanted more, faster and harder, but when I tried to speak, he told me to be silent, and for some reason that sharpened my awareness of what was happening. His hand came round the front and he started fingering my clitoris and at that point I had to remove my hand from my bag and use it to lean on the door to keep my balance. My legs felt as if they would give up and the feeling of him going in and out seemed to invade my body right up to my throat. I could feel my wetness drip down my legs when he pulled back and an exquisite feeling of satisfaction when he pushed in again. I couldn't have found the keys if my life depended on it, and the beauty was I didn't even care.

After we both came we stood a few minutes more, and shaking I finally found the missing key, but I couldn't manage to get it into the lock. Ian took it from me, and still inside me, inserted it into the lock. For some reason this 'insertion' made me horny again and I could feel Ian grow too. He did not pull the door handle down and neither did I, so it all started again, better than the first time.

I never knew nor cared if anyone had seen us, but since that night my neighbour has looked at me in an odd way and started being much more friendly, in an odd and slimy way, so I think it likely he watched at least part of the show. I didn't care because the sex that night, although simple enough in some ways, had contained an extra element that made it one of the most special fucks we ever had.

Ian wanted to contribute to the housekeeping and pay a part of the mortgage as he was living in my house; I let him do the former, but not the latter. Karen kept the small flat she and Ian had shared, and insisted she enjoyed living alone, although she always accepted our dinner invitations willingly. Ian paid part of the expenses for that, telling her it was so he could return there when I threw him out, although he confided to me the main reason was he wanted to help Karen out and would have continued paying it even if he and I were married.

Now I had time to think about something other than the wretched show, I occasionally wondered about Ian and I. We got along really well, each understanding the other, and not just in bed. I liked him as a person and speculated on where our relationship would go after the show finished. Ian would be out of a job, although he could manage the web site and sex call, but what else would he do? If he returned to making porn films I wasn't sure I could accept that comfortably – as time had passed and feelings had become stronger, at least mine had. I wanted him to myself and didn't feel able to share any part of him with anonymous porn ladies. However, the sensible part of me put this to one side, as something to think about when the time came and not worry about before we reached that point.

More worrying was that we were still missing a title for the show, but that came to Ian and I late one night. It had been a particularly hard day when everything went wrong; batteries stopped working, light bulbs blew and too many people phoned in sick at the last minute, with the stomach bug that was doing the rounds. Simon was tetchy, (more than usual), and picked fault with everything all day long, and the contestants were either boring or bad, or indeed both. Those of us fortunate enough to have escaped the twenty-four hour bug, were left with double the work and ended up putting in a fourteen hour day, working at double speed.

That night neither Ian nor I felt like doing wild antics in bed, and after dissecting the day's takes, we decided to skip sex. As I was just about to settle down to try and empty my mind, so I could go to sleep, Ian startled me by saying, "OK, time to sex it up a bit".

I turned to look at him and was just in time to see him perch a pair of glasses I hadn't known existed, on his nose, and opening the drawer in his bedside table, take out a crime novel I also hadn't known was there. He turned and grinned at me, but all I could do was continue to stare. A part of me was shocked to see a sex machine wearing glasses, but another part was processing what he had said.

He mistook my stare for worry, and pointed out he was only joking to make light of his glasses, but having done a few quick calculations I said, "I think that should be the name."

"What should?" he replied.

"Sex It Up!"

He put down the book, took off the owl accessories, and thought for a while.

"It describes the show with the word 'sex' and the 'it' is the classic ambiguous term for having sex, and the 'up' refers to an erect penis, but put together if is quite innocuous and not at all offensive," I explained.

"You know, I think you are right. It is good – and suits well."

At work everyone agreed, or nearly everyone, but most importantly Simon, the big boss, who had the final say, liked it.

The show now had a name, contestants, a venue, a sponsor, judges and was only lacking .... What? I knew there was something I had forgotten, but for now it escaped me.

Ian was keeping an eye on our own products; the fine tuned sex toy chair was being mass produced and we got another one to take home, this meant we now had one each. The web site and VoIP were up and running and we had sponsors for those too. If only I could think of whatever the missing thing was, it would all be complete.

Then as I was mentally running through the whole show, as it would be shown on TV, I realised what was missing – the prize! I hadn't got a major prize yet. I jumped, and Ian asked what was wrong.

That night we ended up sitting in bed talking about sex, but not doing any. We discussed the prize, and talked about a big pot of gold coins, but we were worried about someone pocketing any of them. Pretend gold coins were our compromise. How to show them off was the next puzzle to solve, but between us we had a few brainwaves on that score too.

All along I had wanted to tie this show in with as much other stuff as possible, and had felt the final contestants could make a porn film compilation, while the winners would star in one. Nigel, (one of our judges and porn director), had already set this up.

The contestants had signed a contract stating they would accept 30% of any revenue their appearance generated, and this left us the other 70% to divide with whatever business we were dealing with. In this case, the film people, and in the case of our sex toys sponsor, they would choose a few contestants and name products after them, so there would be 'Sally's Vibrator' and 'John's cock ring', for example. This was all very well, but there needed to be something big and shiny for the winner so we could present it with a flourish on TV. The show needed an ending!

Did we go down the humorous route and present a big gold phallus, or was something more serious better? Then inspiration hit and I suggested someone wheel in a big cake the shape of a penis, and Samantha, the 'diva', present that to the winners. The other contestants could open bottles of Champaign, streamers and glittery stuff, and balloons could fall from above, then the camera would fade out on a party. That was a good ending, but didn't solve the problem of a big prize. Strange no one had realised this was missing, and I wanted to get one in place before Simon caught on to its lack. I would get Jessica on to that first thing tomorrow and hope she managed to convince whatever supplier she found to do a rush job. In the end I needn't have worried, as she got to work immediately and soon knew just where to go for the work. She extracted a promise from the supplier for delivery within a few days, and that was sorted without Simon being any the wiser that this vital part was a rushed afterthought.

Auditions End

The night the auditions ended I came home to find the table set with my best china and crystal glasses. The centrepiece was a beautiful flower arrangement and the whole room was filled with fragrant blooms, while candles supplied the lighting and soft classical music playing, which set the romantic atmosphere very well.

I was surprised at how worried I was that Ian had done this to tell me he was leaving.

"Cocktails or a shower?" he asked softly.

"Cocktails", I replied without hesitation, anxious to hear the reason for our first romantic tryst.

I waited patiently as he poured the drinks, but when he started going through each dish on the menu, I had to interrupt.

"OK Ian, what is the reason for all this? If you want to leave this 'last supper' is a cruel way to do it. "

I am not sure if the look on his face was surprise or pain, but whatever it was, I wanted to remove it by taking back my outburst.

"Is that what you think of me?" he whispered.

This was the tine for honesty if I was to have any chance of a future with this man – and that was what I wanted.

"No, it is what I fear, as I have come to care for you so much."

Saying nothing he bounded over and took me in his arms, and we stayed that way for quite a while.

When we did release each other, he called me a silly girl and told me to sit down and listen.

"This dinner was because I wanted to talk to you about us. We have sort of drifted into being together and I wanted to make it official. I was going to leave it up to you whether we continued living here or bought a new house together. Both suit me, all I want is you."

Delighted and relieved, I went to him and hugged him, then we sat holding hands for a while. This was a new step for us, as we had done the whole thing back to front. Sex first and romance later, but that had suited us both.

Dinner was wonderful, and as Ian had not been needed in the studios that day, he had spent all day cooking. We ate three courses of delicate vichyssoise, filo wrapped pork, stuffed with red pesto and served with asparagus, glazed baby carrots and hazelnut crusted courgettes, and finally a chocolate fondant with a raspberry sauce. It was as good as any top restaurant would serve, and Ian had made such an effort for this dinner, I felt something as close to love as I could ever remember feeling.

After coffee and brandy I went and ran a bath, and as I too had been thinking about going down a more romantic route, I dug out a special packet I had bought on impulse a few days earlier and had hidden until the time was right. While the bath tub was filling I collected and lit candles, placing them around the room and lit oil burners with Ylang Ylang, (both relaxing and considered an aphrodisiac), then I opened the special bag and sprinkled the bath with fragrant rose petals in hues of pink. I set Air on a G String on continuous play and called Ian. He came in, looked round and again took me in his arms. Granted I had set a rather romantic scene, but then so had he, and there was nothing to say good sex cannot come out of romance too.

I stripped slowly, never taking my eyes away from his and lowered myself into the water, then watched as he too removed his clothes. I was delighted to see he was already very hard, as I was extremely wet, and it had nothing to do with the bath water. I was throbbing in time to the music and Ian had yet to touch me. There were no toys and no extras, but I was as excited as I had ever been, and judging by Ian's erection he too felt that magic 'it' in the air. What happened next is something I feel shouldn't be discussed as it was the most intimate thing we have done and it feels wrong to make it public. Suffice to say, what we did was probably closer to making love than to having sex, but it was just as good and our organisms were long and mind-blowing.

I think I can say this was the best sex I have ever had and strangely, for me, it was also the most uncomplicated too. I can highly recommend it.

The Finalists

Our eight couples for the finals were finally complete. Philip and Joan, the shy couple who shagged like horny rabbits; Claude, the Italian stallion and his wife Fiona, (his real name was Fred and someone should have told him Claude was a French name, not Italian); Andrew with his fabulous voice and his wife Deborah; Susan, who liked to be called Suzanna, (with a 'z'), as it better suited her smouldering image and her partner Andrew who came to be called Andy to avoid confusion with the other Andrew.

Amanda, (Mandy), arrived in a twin set and pearls – really – and her husband Luke proudly presented his best plus-fours and a deerstalker as his attire. They lived in a big old house in the country and regularly had tea with the vicar. The idea behind their dress code was to shock – and it worked. Many people describe country women as looking like a horse, but Mandy was more like a rabbit, buck teeth and all, but it appears these work to your advantage for giving blow jobs as you can gently scrap your teeth down the man's shaft to give pleasure – who knew! Their sex show was the antipathy of their languid demeanour; lively and animated. There was little to stand out except the fact they were rather genteel folk and you do not expect a lady to yell, "Fuck me harder," in a posh voice, or a gentleman to drawl, "Bend over bitch so I can ram your ass." At the moment of orgasm Mandy screamed really loudly, while a protracted "Agggggggh" came from Luke in a deep rumble.

The husband and wife team of Tom and Shelia and the partners that were John and Frank, (Frank was the man who had come as a threesome and we had tried him with John for the show), were all normal to look at. The sort of people you would not notice in a crowd. John and Frank were gentle and loving and concentrated on pleasuring each other fully and completely. It was sweet and sensual to watch and had caused a debate amongst the judges about whether their performance was different enough to warrant a place in the final. To be honest, they made it on my say so, only because they were different to the others, not just because they were the only gay couple, but also because of the romantic element. Initially they had whispered sweet nothings to each other, but we had to ask them to speak up so the audience could hear, and this seemed to put them off a bit as there was little talking after that. We had suffered a scarcity of couples who were interesting enough, and as we put John and Frank into the final, I wondered if their act was all just for show, or if we had contributed to making a new happy couple.

Tom and Shelia went down the soft bondage route, with him leading her to the table and placing objects in her hand which she looked at and carefully felt and caressed, then he blindfolded her, removed the toys from her hands, and made her describe what she thought he had inserted into her opening. She then described what she wanted, bigger, longer and so on. The roles were reversed and she tied his hands to the high ring suspended from the roof and repeated the process using cock rings, anal beads and other items. The foreplay over, they were both so ready for sex the actual act did not last long, but the protracted games at the beginning were enough to see them through to the final.

Pete and Mary only stood out for their frantic behaviour. They used every single toy and accessory provided, jumping from one thing to another wildly depending on the shouted “Yes” or “no” their partner provided. It was a fun show rather than an exciting one, but variety is not only the spice of life, it is also the seasoning to a good TV show, so we put them into the live final, excited to see what they would make of a whole house full of toys.

Live Final

Having got my own way about filming the finals in the villa, I was now worried it would not work. There was no surer way to get fired than to make the company spend a lot of money for something that failed. Also, as these shows were live, if they were not interesting it would make the whole show a flop, and not too many producers manage to stay employed after a major disaster, especially newly promoted ones.

I needn't have worried. The show was a total success with everyone behaving well most of the time. The aging film star was in her element, just as we had all suspected, and she had even used part of the money we paid her to buy herself a 'throne-like' chair from which she summonsed people willy-nilly. She asked probing questions and generally brought out sides of the contestants the public would otherwise not have seen. Tact was not her strong point and on more than one occasion she provoked women into crying and men into losing their temper, but it was all part of the human interest we were looking for.

I had given Samantha a brief that said we wanted to find out personal details, secrets, sexual fantasies and anything else, but how she went about this and what else she found out was up to her. Luckily I had put her through a trial run with Ian and Karen, neither of whom she had met. She tended to harangue them and not much more, but once I told her to look at it as if she were playing the part of a talk show host, like Johnny Carson, Michael Parkinson and Oprah Winfrey –with much more attitude, and more probing, but to be better than them, (to appeal to her vanity), she really threw herself into it, and immediately started her interrogations.

She delved so deep, Tom and Shelia found out things about their partner they didn't know, and they split up there and then. She did this spying so effortlessly too, which made it even more of a surprise.

As they walked into her throne room they both said "Hello."

"Sit down" was the only reply.

Once they were seated Samantha launched straight into the strong stuff; "Why did you enter this show? Was it because you like sex or money?"

"Well, we..." Tom began.

"I will interrupt you there, as I am not sure what makes you think you are qualified to talk about your wife's feelings, so please tell me why *you* did it and your wife will tell me her reasons herself."

"Right," and we could see Tom struggling to keep control of his temper, "Well, em..."

"Do hurry up. I haven't got all day. There are other people to interview and *they* have interesting things to say."

"It was the money", Tom said in hushed tones.

"And you?" rounding on Shelia.

"The sex", and at that Tom stared at his wife in surprise.

"So I assume that means you don't get enough good sex at home?"

"Yes, I mean, no."

"Which is it? If you had enough sex at home you wouldn't have come here."

"Well, we do have lots of sex, but I just wanted a bit more."

Samantha probed a bit more before throwing a big spanner into the works by asking for no apparent reason, "I hope you use a vibrator rather than cheat on your husband when you want extra thrills?"

"Yes, of course!"

Tom whipped round, angry. "What do you mean you use a vibrator? I should be enough!"

"Oh, don't be so daft. You are useless and every time you go to have a shower after sex, I finish what you couldn't, with my trusty vibrator."

Samantha had the sense to leave them to it, and she sat back quietly as they tore each other to pieces.

Tom got so indignant about the slur on his manhood he tried to prove the fault was not with him by explaining;

"John has never complained and I have had much more sex with him than with you."

"John? Who the hell is John?" Shelia queried.

"My best friend John – you needn't pretend you don't know him. He often comes for dinner."

"By the sound of things he *comes* for much more than dinner."

It all came out that Tom and John had started a relationship at school and had continued it even after Tom's marriage. A huge verbal slanging match broke out and Samantha struggled to regain control of the situation, without success. Both partners walked out in a rage, so I sent Karen to try and persuade them to continue for the prize money, and her gentle ways got exactly the result we wanted.

Suzanna and Andy were also a revelation. Samantha asked Suzanna what she had brought her partner for, as she did everything herself. The reply started off innocuous enough but this too soon turned into quite a scene.

"This show is for couples, so I needed another person and Andy agreed to accompany me."

"Why do you think he agreed?"

"I told him I would tell dad if he didn't!"

"And what would your father say if you told him?" Samantha was astute enough not to ask outright what could have been told.

"He would see it as incest, of course."

This had me on my feet instantly, but Ian and Jessica stopped me, by suggesting we let the whole interview run its course. I was just glad this part was not live, and we could hold it back.

"You obviously don't see it as incest, so could you not explain it to him?"

"He won't listen. He sees that bitch he married as sacred and everything regarding her is untouchable, so he would blame me for corrupting Andy."

"Why don't you use this interview to put your point of view across? It is a great opportunity to explain to everyone why you are right."

That is what Suzanna did. Andy was her step brother, (her father married again and Andy was his wife's son from her first marriage), and while technically not a relation, and therefore perfectly legal, with no incest as such, it did provide a certain extra interest in this pair.

The participants, on the whole, behaved as we had hoped, having sex in random places; on the beach, in the sea, on small boats pulled onto the sand, (with missing oars so we had no 'out to sea' disasters), in all the rooms in the house, in the bath and shower and on the kitchen table just before dinner, and one evening after a boozy barbeque – an orgy. We couldn't have planned it better if we had tried – although actually, that was what I had planned for – setting it up so they could have a group bang, and crossing my fingers. It was not a wild, frenzied random coupling, but more as if each person was keen to find out what the competition did. I would love to have seen 'the voice' with 'the siren', but probably because both were the sexual leaders, this did not happen. However this gave me an idea for next year's show if we did it again, and if this were the success it seemed, we would be doing it for many years to come. My idea was to get couples to swap and then rate each other, but I would have to find some criteria to stop them all automatically giving low marks to others, in the hope they would win themselves. Luckily both Ian and Karen were good at coming up with ideas and if we sat down together something was sure to work. I would have to keep it a secret meeting or to invite Jessica as well, so as not to insult her. She was a great worker and assistant, but had no creative thoughts at all. She was a follower and would never be a leader – I don't think she wanted to be either, as one of her favourite remarks was 'just tell me what to do and I will do it – at least then I don't have to think.' Anyway plenty of time to sort out details for next year, and I had to make sure this year worked perfectly first.

We had got chocolate dildos which I had thought the contestants could lick and eat to stimulate each other, but one couple went even further. She actually used it, and surprisingly it did not break or melt much, and when she had finished she gave it to him and he sucked and ate it. He then licked the chocolate from her opening as a finale. (The company who made it said they were inundated with orders for chocolate penises after that show and had trouble keeping up with production.)

I noticed a few contestants had shaved their genital area in the few weeks between auditions and finals. We had only put through one shaved lady and one man, (Tom and Mary), but we now had four men and two ladies with private parts that looked the way they did when they were born. Suzanna and Andy, Frank and Claude had all visited a 'hairdresser' at some point before coming to the tropical island.

Suzanna and Claude had also added piercing to their art in the seven weeks between their audition and the live show. He had multiple bars on the side of his shaft and she had a vertical clitoris piercing, both piercings chosen for the heightened sexual pleasure they reportedly gave. She also had brightly coloured ribbons and a feather hanging from a vaginal piercing with a bell on it too. This was actually amazing as it rang with a delicate tinkle every time her clitoris was touched and when she climaxed it make a song all its own. These were things I personally had no desire to try – I had too much respect for my private parts to subject them to this invitation or infection – and I would try just about anything, but each to their own.

In theory every participant had signed a contract stating they would not change anything about their genital area before filming began, and some sponsors and crew wanted these people removed. I wasn't happy about these modifications, but the fact was, we had struggled to get enough contestants good enough to fill all the slots, so by dropping half of them – we probably would not be able to fill their places at this late stage.

I reached a compromise which everyone was happy with, well not strictly happy, but willing to accept. The contestants signed a waiver forfeiting 50% of any money, sponsorship deals or rewards of any type that came out of their participating, but they stayed in the show.

The sponsors agreed quite willingly, as they would save money, and the crew saw the difficulty in replacing these people at this point and acquiesced. As far as the participants were concerned; when faced with the alternative of – either accept willingly, with no huffing, (there had been quite a bit of that), or we will sue you for breach of contract – they accepted, although 'willingly' is not a word I would use to describe their acceptance. 'If we feel you are in any way sulking we will still sue you' was added, and they accepted, signing a new contract. I heard a lot of complaints behind the scenes, but for the camera they behaved well enough, and that was what counted.

Our viewing numbers started out all right, but they grew massively as the show continued and were close behind the biggest and longest running reality show numbers before the last few episodes. The public voted in their millions and, although we had given the judges a vote which counted for 33% of the total, this was more to let the public know what experts thought, rather than to influence the outcome. The judges voted immediately the intercourse was over and when all the couples had shagged we showed ten minutes of audition clips to give the public time to vote, then it was the classic eliminations.

Although we did not announce the actual number of votes we did make a big thing of each week's winners, and obviously the losers too, as they were sent home.

The first show was the participants more or less repeating their auditions, and Andrew and Deborah won, with Mandy and Luke second, John and Frank third and Claude and Fiona sent home, much to Claude's shouted chagrin. I would have thought Suzanna and Andy would have been higher than sixth, but I assumed most of our voters must have been women and the 'siren act' most certainly appeals more to men.

Week two Andrew and Deborah won again, although his 'talk' about Debs 'mounting a horse and feeling the horse between her legs' didn't do it for me at all. I thought it just sounded wrong on every level, but I was in the minority. Pete and Mary went home as, having already used all the toys, they seemed at a bit of a loss what else to do, and simply repeated the same wild dash for another implement. Word must have spread about Suzanna as she and Andy were second this time, even though her repertoire seemed limited to the same scene, but this time he did stick his cock into her briefly at the end. It looked like he came, as indicated by a short grunt, but she didn't seem to achieve satisfaction. With John and Frank third again, they and Andrew seemed to have fond a faithful following. Philip and Joan had been seventh the last time and their shy entrance and frantic coupling and screaming barely saved them this week as they were again close to leaving, in sixth place.

I needed to have a chat with all the contestants and set up a meeting for the day after the show. Andrew and Deborah were the only ones to change their performance, and even they did the same thing, just using a different setting, so I told the others they needed to do something different if they wanted to continue in the show. I threatened to let more than one couple go home unless it got more interesting, (I had got a clause in the contract that said we could change the rules any time we wanted, but I didn't intend to let more than one pair go – it was just a rouse to gee them up a bit), and I suggested they spend the week thinking of something new.

The filming that day was no use to us as they all analysed their performance and discussed what they could do in a clinical way, so I sent Jessica in to remind them they were being filmed for the show all week, and not just on the live performance, so to make the talk sexier and inspiring, and not a clinical analysis.

Things were looking a bit bleak until the following day when Tom and Shelia asked to speak to me. They wanted to use the Joystick Vibrator Chair® and wondered if they could have a hangman's hood so one of them could pretend to be an executioner, strapping the other into the electric chair. It sounded a bit risqué but when I ran it past the legal department they said, 'provided no one mentioned the words electric chair it was fine,' so I got them their hood.

The performance they gave – he 'captured' her a short distance from the chair, tied her and blindfolded her, before pushing her onto a bed and using a dildo on her for a short while. Then he led her to the chair, where she acted as if it were the real electric chair. He strapped her in and asked if she were ready before turning it on and we all watched the big phallus rise up and enter her. She gave a great performance with loads of 'ohs' and 'ahs', and also lots of 'no, enough, please stop,' as the chair pulsed and vibrated, moving in and out of her wet pussy. He gently played with himself while she suffered the delights the chair offered, as if getting off on her suffering, (and maybe he really did), and she came before he did. When he stopped the chair she begged for more and he retaliated by saying he would give her more the next day if she became his slave and did everything for him. She acquiesced and once released gave him a blow job before straddling him on the ground and riding his shaft while working his testicles, and all purely for his pleasure.

All of this took them into first place that week and voting figures for the others rose too – all except Philip and Joan who didn't really change their intercourse and who went home.

I think this inventiveness and resulting votes for Tom and Shelia inspired the rest of the contestants as, from then on things got better and changed more.

I had thought of setting up a 'warn up room' so the next contestants could do whatever it took to get them wet and hard, and when a shag lasted too long we switched view to the warm up room to show a bit of that too, to alleviate the boredom. The warm ups seemed to mainly consist of pornographic magazines and vibrators, but one couple believed if they had an orgasm before going in they could do better inside the main room, so we were treated to them having quick sex, oral sex and anything else to achieve a hurried but intentionally small climax.

Contestants were sent home, and numbers dwindled, and to use up more time we encouraged more foreplay. I brought in a mini quiz; each contestant was asked to rate 'how it was for them' on a scale of 1 – 10, and then their partners were asked how they thought the other party felt. The results were interesting and varied. The majority feeling they had performed better than their partners felt they had, and this provoked defensive arguments and more effort to get a better mark. This was not part of the voting as such, just a time filler, but again it let the public see more of the characters of the people involved.

During the next show Mandy and Luke did a scene where he came home and told her he had invited four business associates for a long weekend in the country. He asked her what she would give them to eat, and then in a suggestive voice asked how she would entertain them by going through a list of the guest's names.

"Mr Jordan is an investment banker and wears a bow tie. How do you intend to make him happy? Show me," Luke demanded, and sat down in an arm chair. Mandy started to strip while touching herself.

When she had finished Luke said, "Yes. I think he will like that."

"Now Mr Meers is a lawyer, what about him?"

Mandy took Luke's hand and led him to the bed where she undressed him and tied him to the bed posts before working him into a frenzy with her hands and mouth around his genital area, but never touching his penis. When she released him the 'trial run' for Mr Adams followed, and involved Mandy being demure and allowing Mr Adams to take advantage of her by only struggling weakly and therefore inflaming him more.

'Mr Browne' was a work of art in its own way, with desperate and rough sex. He rammed powerfully into her and she yelled 'harder, more' and as things were working towards orgasm he pulled back for a big thrust – she moved and he missed. He looked startled and we all wondered what had happened, but it wasn't long before she said, "You will give my husband the work, won't you?"

"What?" he screamed as his angry penis stood to attention.

She turned onto her stomach and kept her legs closed, "I will let you use my other, tighter opening", was her answer. His face showed delight and a quick, "Yes, of course, whatever," was all it took for her legs to spread and allow him to penetrate her anus.

This spectacle catapulted them into first place and again inspired the others into more role playing too, as the sex hotted up. Andrew and Deborah and Suzanna and Andy replayed more or less the same things, although Andrew did change the location again, and both pairs scrapped through, although with low votes. John and Frank, with the least votes, went home.

Tom and Shelia stayed in second place for the next show with another bondage type seduction. Their strength was more in how they used the scene, rather than acting out a part. What I mean is; he picked her up somewhere and invited her back to his house. He then produced his handcuffs and she tried to leave, so he cuffed her to a post we had placed for that purpose, (or for a pole dance). She didn't really struggle or act frightened, but succumbed to him blindfolding her without a word and from then on the only sound to pass her lips were gasps and 'ohs' as he fingered her, massaged her clitoris and used butt plugs, anal beads and a variety of vibrators and wands. When he released her they moved to the bed and finished there.

As the crew rushed in to change the sheets, I speculated on what Suzanna would do this time. If she didn't make more of an effort I thought, (and secretly hoped), she would be going home. My wish was granted, and the following show Andrew's 'voice over' failed to excite viewers sufficiently and he too went home.

The final then was between two opposites, Mandy and Luke's twin set and pearls and Tom and Shelia's bondage.

Eventually we ended up with a winner and a runner up, and none of us workers would have chosen the winner, I would even go so far as to say they were our least likely candidates. Their personality wasn't great, and this made for boring foreplay after you had seen it a few times. The sex was generally pretty straight too, him on top, her on top, bent over a chair, a little bondage, some use of our Joystick Vibrator Chair® and other toys, but his dick was huge – massive, unbelievable, and she took it anywhere and everywhere she could, so maybe that was why. It may also have been the 'shock factor', hearing such a posh accent, viewers certainly didn't expect vulgarities to come out in a woolly accent, but again there was little 'shock' after you had seen them a few times.

Some of us had thought Tom and Shelia, the runners up, would win. They were inventive and innovative. She bent him over a chair and used a dildo on him; he bent her double and tied her wrists to her ankles before fucking both orifices; he put a bar of chocolate in her vagina and ate it and to follow an open bottle of fizzy cola. She covered his already hard penis in honey and sprinkled chocolate bits on it, blindfolded him and left him for a short while. Then she returned with a feather and slowly tortured him by touching his balls and anus. He kept shouting he was going to explode, and when that happened she drew ice cubs over his testicles and things subsided a bit. (Ian and I got hours of pleasure back in our hotel room each day this was couple on). Perhaps their bondage scenes, even though not too heavy, were too much for many voters – who knows.

Award Speeches

We were nominated for a couple of TV's top awards; 'Best New Reality Show' and 'Best Production'. I called a meeting, so we could choose who to send to the dinner in the four places allocated to us. As producer I would have to go, but Simon would expect to be there too if we won, so it was decided Simon, Jessica and I would go from the production side, and Ian from the judges, (he was the best looking, least vulgar and porn like, of the three).

Before we got dressed to go to the ceremony Ian gave me a beautifully wrapped present. It was one of those ones where you want to try and open it slowly so you do not ruin the presentation, but Ian wanted me to hurry. I compromised and only ripped the ends of the paper – to find a plain cardboard box inside. Opening this produced a small purple, silicone vibrator – with a remote control.

"Wear this tonight, please."

I was already wet thinking about what fun this would be, but a thought struck me and I said, "I will wear it on one condition – you do not leave me hanging on the brink of orgasm and then switch the thing off. Tonight is too important to me to be left in that horrible place where I am unsatisfied and my mind stops working until my pussy is filled."

"Deal, but I can tease you lots before then, right?"

"Oh, yes please!"

I put it on and we tested it immediately, and as Ian had said, it was remarkable quiet. The sensation was lovely, but gentle, and that meant we would get hours of fun from it that evening. The thought of using a vibrator in front of everyone, without them knowing, gave me a huge buzz – and thinking about going shopping with it hidden under my cloths added to my excitement.

We sat through long speeches where every winner thanked each person on the planet separately, and our own nomination of 'Best New Reality Show' failed to secure the coveted trophy. Many times I had to hold back a moan, and looking at Ian, which I didn't often do as it got me more worked up, I could see he was taking pleasure in being the cause of my discomfort. I wondered if my own face was as flushed and odd looking as his was, and hoped not, while suspecting it was. Luckily the excitement of the awards ceremony could be thought to be responsible and I believed no one would guess the real reason.

Towards the end of the evening and of my reserves of control, (as Ian had used the remote freely and piteously all night, but stopped each time before letting me build up to orgasm), the winner of 'Best Production' was announced – and it was me. I don't know if it was luck, or incredible calculation on Ian's part, but the announcement coincided with Ian finally giving me a climax, so when my name was called I gave an unusually loud and enthusiastic "Yes" before we all trudged onto the stage.

I spoke first, trying to keep it short and passed over to Simon who rambled on for ages. Jessica smiled and Ian stepped up to the microphone.

"Working on this show was great fun and an eye opener about just how much detail there is to keep under control. Kate was incredible and spending so much time with her I came to realise one thing..." He paused for a long time while never taking his eyes off me. My already overworked heart took this opportunity to stop and I felt sick. What was he going to say?

He dropped onto one knee.

Oh Hell, no I thought and tried to catch his eye and stop this before it went too far.

"Katie, will you marry me?"

The place erupted. I thought I was going to pass out, and hoped this would indeed happen as it was an easy way out. It didn't.

I knew I couldn't stand there in silence, so walked over to him, bent down and kissed him, saying in as sexy a voice as I could manage, "I'll give you my answer later, when we are alone."

I was vaguely aware of some applause, but this was drowned out by boos and hisses. I threw Simon a desperate pleading look and, to my astonishment, he obliged by hustling us all off the stage. Back in our seats I knew Ian must be feeling bad and tried to make things better by saying, "I thought you liked things the way they are?"

"You thought wrong, wouldn't you say, otherwise I would not have made such an idiot of myself on national TV?"

We couldn't talk about it there – we were surrounded by people, there was too much noise and we couldn't see each other's faces and expressions. It would have to wait until we got home.

However, once home it seemed there was nothing to talk about.

Ian started packing his bags and refused to discuss it.

At first I tried pointing out I didn't want our relationship to stop, I just wasn't ready for it to move onto another plane, but as he pushed past me to reach things and would not utter one single word, I eventually lost my temper.

"We have never declared love for each other, never talked about marriage or anything much that is a serious subject – you know I value my privacy very, very much, so how could you think it was a good idea to propose like that?" I screamed.

"I take it back. I proposed to the person I thought you were, but not to the person you really are. I have no wish to be around that person, let alone be tied to her for the rest of my life. If you agree we will keep our business interests and Jack can act as go between so we don't have to meet. I will get Karen another job, so I am officially giving you her notice and I will send someone round to get the rest of my stuff."

And he walked out of my life.

I thought about what had happened a lot after that night, but although I suffered from his absence and missed him, I did feel I had done the right thing. The niggling question though, was what I would have said had he asked me in private.

I had often expressed my dismay and dislike of public 'I love yous', and every time one of the contestants said it, I remarked how inappropriate it was and how strongly I felt 'I love you' was a private and intimate thing and not to be declared in public. I had also made it very clear I felt my private life should be just that – private. Working in the television media let me see a lot of things happen publicly, (and this included the programmes I organised), that I felt were more suited to closed doors, but if others wished to do it or enjoyed watching, that was fine – it just wasn't for me. Everyone who worked with me had got this, and even joked about it, saying the way I protected my privacy was like a mother bear protecting her baby bear.

Yet, Ian choose to propose in as public manner as possible, and while part of me was embarrassed, the biggest worry was how much it showed Ian did not understand me and had not listened to me whenever I expressed repugnance at the new fashion of making the general public a part of your private life.

Karen showed up for work the next day and asked to talk to me in private. She said Ian had returned to the flat the night before and refused to talk to her, but before closing himself in his room he had told her he had resigned on her behalf. She was furious with him and told him so, and they too had had a blazing row and weren't speaking.

She did want to continue working with me, if I could bear to have her there, and as she had done nothing wrong, I stated I would like that very much.

I had believed I was professional enough to deal with her presence, but I had not reckoned with my out of control emotions and every time I looked at her I saw Ian. A part of me was dying to ask what he was doing, and a part was afraid he had moved on and had another woman and I was just a distant blot on his horizon. Karen and I both danced round the topic and carefully did not include his name in our talks, but it was there nonetheless, and stayed hovering over our heads.

By now the company had moved on to producing a drama and a cookery show was scheduled to follow. Neither of these were my idea, but I was in charge of them nonetheless, and while the drama was good and stood on its own feet, the cookery show was keeping me busy as it was dull, dull and even duller. Short of having everyone strip and cook naked, I could find no way to brighten up a show that had been done too many times by our rivals, and any spare time I had was spent watching every one of these episode to try and fine the angle we needed.

Perhaps the problem was I found concentration hard, as my thoughts kept wandering to Ian and my body was complaining far too much about a lack of sex. I couldn't do anything about the first and didn't feel like doing anything about the second, so instead, tried to come to terms with living with these emotions.

I missed Ian, not just in my bed, although my body trembled with lack of sex, but also talking to him and having him around. I wished he had left things as they were, or at least had asked me in private, although I had to admit to myself I still didn't know what answer I would have given. The public display seemed like a betrayal, as I had told him so very often how much I hated anyone showing feelings in public. A part of me knew I should feel honoured he had wanted to publicly declare his love, but the truth was I felt belittled, humiliated, embarrassed and betrayed. I wished we could go back to the way things had been, but knew from the way Ian had left me, that if anything were to happen it would have to be him make the first move. I had tried one phone call, but he hung up as soon as he had established the call was not about work. If I went to him he would see it as pity in his frame of mind, so all I could do was hope, but get on with life.

Late for Work

Then one day Karen didn't show up for work. She had now been with me for thirteen months, (seven of those while I was with Ian), and had never been late, never had a day off sick and always told me where she would be and when she would be back, so I knew something was wrong.

I got Jessica to phone the flat, (I didn't want to risk Ian answering as he would hear how worried I was, and Karen was not answering her mobile), but she returned to say Ian was worried because Karen had left to come into the office at the normal time.

Between Jessica and I, we kept ringing Karen's mobile, hoping she would pick up, and at nearly eleven o'clock a white faced Jessica came in and sat down opposite me.

"I rang Karen's phone and a man answered", she said.

"And?" I prompted, as this did not seem like a good enough reason for Karen to not turn up and for Jessica's pallor.

"He said he was a doctor."

"And?" I prompted again.

"Karen had an accident this morning and she is in hospital."

"Where?" I asked and quickly realised there was a more important question.

"How is she?"

"She is in a coma and has head injuries. He doesn't think she will live through today."

I felt like I was going to fall over, but as I was sitting down this seemed unlikely, but I also felt that I was going to be sick, and as this really seemed probable I dashed to the toilet, where my prophecy came true.

When I had got myself cleaned up I went back to my office to find Jessica still there.

"Right," I said as I grabbed my handbag. "Phone Ian in case he doesn't know. I'm going there now."

"It's St Mary's," Jessica shouted as I was leaving.

Just as well, as I was on my way to visit a hospital without knowing which to go to. I was relieved it was that one, as it really was close by and I could be there in no time.

I arrived before Ian, which was no surprise as he had to cross from almost the other side of town, and I lied my way into her room – it was family only, so I said I was her sister-in-law.

She lay like an angel between huge machines, tubes and bandages, and in reality looked dead. I sat beside her and took her hand. "What happened," I asked the question more to destiny, than Karen herself, and burst into tears.

I didn't hear Ian come in and saw him when I lifted my head. He was on Karen's other side, doing exactly what I was doing – holding her hand and crying. I felt my heart breaking so much I didn't think I could stand it. It was breaking for Karen and for the suffering Ian was going through.

I got up and going round behind him put my arms round him. He didn't move, but I kept hugging him, trying to give him some of my strength to help him.

After a while I asked if he wanted to be alone with her, but he shook his head, so I sat back down on the other side again.

At one point a doctor came in and asked to speak to Ian, offering to let Ian's wife come too. I had forgotten the small detail of my lie, but Ian said nothing, and just held out his hand. I got up and taking it we followed the doctor to his room.

"She had a severe blow to the head, but there is no internal bleeding. The only other damage is a few cracked ribs and a broken wrist. She was in a coma when the ambulance got there and there is nothing we can do. She has to fight this herself and whether she comes out of it or not, depends on her own will to live."

Ian said nothing, so I asked, "Can we talk her out of it? Can she hear?"

"There is no scientific proof that patients in a coma can hear, but many doctors believe they can. I think talking to her could do some good – it certainly can't do any harm. The next few hours are critical. She can come out of it, stay stable or degenerate in that time, and obviously which of these happens is what will determine her future."

There was little else to say, so we left the white coated man and headed back towards her room. Ian had not spoken at all since we met the doctor and seemed to be in a silent trance. He was no help to

Karen like that, and on the way back to her room I had an idea.

"You need a cup of coffee, and don't argue. You are no use to Karen like this, so we will go to the café and you can pull yourself together before going back," I stated, expecting an argument.

Instead, Ian changed course and headed for the café. He sat at the first table available, just inside the door and I went to get the drinks. Why these places don't sell brandy I don't know. That was what he needed more than instant, powered coffee, but it would have to do for now.

I tried to reason him out of this deep depression for Karen's sake, but to no avail, and eventually ended up on my feet screaming at him about how selfish he was, always thinking of himself. I had intended to simply try and provoke a reaction but once I started I seemed unable to stop and added, "That is what you did to me too. You asked me publicly because it was what you wanted, not what I wanted, and if you had ever listened to me you would have known that. Right now Karen needs you, so put aside your own despair for a while and be there for her."

What came out of my mouth may not have been exactly what I had intended, but the reaction was exactly the one I had been going for.

"I have always been there for Karen! You wouldn't know anything about it, 'miss no emotion'. I am going back to her room and I would be grateful if you didn't come."

He stood up and left.

At least he was speaking again, and hopefully would talk to Karen.

Not feeling like facing everyone at work, and besides there was nothing to tell them yet, I walked into a park and sat down on a bench for a few minutes.

Sometime later there was a noise which started to annoy me, and it took quite a feat of mental energy to recognise it as my phone.

I answered to find an agitated Jessica asking 'where the hell I was'. Karen had regained consciousness an hour ago and would be fine. Ian had phoned looking for me and had left a message for me to visit her.

I looked at my watch – 4.40pm! What had happened? Had I been sitting there for hours? I supposed I must have been. I don't know what time I had left the hospital, but it must have been around 1 – 1.30pm. No wonder my back was stiff and I was cold.

I went back to the ward, delighted Karen would be all right, but anxious about Ian. Had he left? Would he be there? What would he say?

He was there and said little. We just sat talking quietly to Karen, hearing how a lorry had pulled out of a side road and rammed her before she had time to swerve out of the way.

She apologised for being late and asked if she still had a job. I reassured her on that and she proclaimed tiredness and a need to sleep, suggesting we went home, but not before we had talked.

Ian wanted us to get a cup of coffee in the hospital café again, but I preferred a nearby coffee shop as it was more private and less depressing, and we went there. Only after we had finished our coffee did Ian say anything other than to talk about his sister.

He missed me, and I admitted to missing him too. He still wanted to marry me – I still didn't feel like making such a commitment, especially after our bust up. Ian asked if there was any way we could compromise and I replied that living together, just like before, was as close to marriage as you could get, and I would like that, if he were willing.

He was, and we did.

Meanwhile, back at work, Jessica related how speculation was rife in the office. Everyone had known Ian and I were having an affair during the show and when we split up they just assumed it was a TV romance for me, destined to last only as long as the programme. Apparently when I had hysterically insisted Jessica tell Ian about Karen's accident, they had all thought he had dumped me for her and wondered how I managed to still be so nice to her.

I put them straight, explaining it all, although I still let them think Ian and I had got together during the show, and not before. By now Karen had proved she was able to do the job well and everyone liked her, so no one would mind that she was Ian's sister.

Things quickly got back to normal and Karen recovered totally with amazing speed. When Jessica left to have a baby and become a stay-at-home mum, I promoted Karen to take Jessica's place.

Our web site, Joystick Vibrator Chair® and video phone business thrive, providing us with enough money to give up work if we wish. Ian and I live together happily and the show became a block-buster with a regular yearly series. We didn't give up work, but limited ourselves to mainly working on 'Sex it Up' and the four spin-off shows, all my ideas; one was after the show finished we follow the winners and make a documentary on their one to two months following their win, to see how it changed their lives; another was masturbation championships; world record breaking sex, (either longest lasting, more partners, most cocks in one vagina or any other record we could break), and non-heterosexual sex - and every year, between the shows, we took time off to travel or just laze at home and have sex.

Ian and I still experiment with sex, but truth to tell, there is not much left that we haven't already tried. We live in hope that someone somewhere, will have a new idea we can play with.

www.ingramcontent.com/pod-product-compliance
Ingram Content Group UK Ltd.
Pitfield, Milton Keynes, MK11 3LW, UK
UKHW020219250726
13967UKWH00001B/87

9 781291 502435